GW01270581

FORGIVENESS

10 studies
for individuals or groups

Christine Platt

With Notes for Leaders

SCRIPTURE UNION

Scripture Union, 207–209 Queensway, Bletchley, MK2 2EB, England.
email: info@scriptureunion.org.uk
Internet: http://www.scripture.org.uk/

First published 1999

ISBN 1 85999 347 8

British Library Cataloguing-in-Publication Data
A catalogue record for this book is available from the British Library.

Cover design: InterVarsity Press/ie Design.
Printed and bound in Great Britain by Ebenezer Baylis & Son Limited, The Trinity Press, Worcester and London.

Contents

Getting the Most Out of *Forgiveness*

Forgiveness is an incredible gift and a mighty mystery. How can a holy God overlook sin, especially when I do the same thing over and over again? Doesn't my sin diminish him as God? Does he relegate me to the back row of his chosen people? Does he get fed up with forgiving me time and time again? What is his attitude towards me when I talk to him about my failures — impatient, bored, exasperated, loving?

Even though many of us believe the Bible is true and could quote verses about forgiveness, we find ourselves labouring under a load of guilt — mistakes we've made; angry, spiteful words we've uttered. Yet God promises his children freedom from guilt and condemnation. If we really grasped the wonder of being forgiven, being clean and holy, surely we would praise God more and our faces and lifestyle would radiate joy and gratitude.

For those who have been acutely hurt by others, to contemplate forgiving them seems an almost impossible task. We know that to hold grudges and allow resentment to fester is harmful physically, emotionally and spiritually, but pain can go so deep that it feels as though nothing can heal the wound.

What hope and help does the Bible hold out for people in these situations?

In these studies, we will look at the experiences of people such as the adulterous woman, David and Joseph, to discover principles and examples to help us grow in our understanding and experience of being forgiven and forgiving others. Needless to say, while on this earth we will never fully plumb the depths or scale the heights of what forgiveness is all about. That amazing experience awaits us when we get to heaven and see Jesus face to face! But our heavenly Father wants us to live today in the light of his forgiveness, for which he and his Son paid so dearly.

Suggestions for Individual Study

1. As you begin each study, pray that God will speak to you through his Word.

2. Read the introduction to the study and respond to the "personal reflection" question or exercise. This is designed to help you focus on God and on the theme of the study.

3. Each study deals with a particular passage, so that you can delve into the author's meaning in that context. Read and reread the passage to be studied. If you are studying a book, it will be helpful to read through the entire book prior to the first study. The questions are written using the language of the New International Version, so you may wish to use that version of the Bible. The New Revised Standard Version is also recommended.

4. This is an inductive Bible study, designed to help you discover for yourself what Scripture is saying. The study includes three types of question. *Observation* questions ask about the basic facts: who, what, when, where and how. *Interpretation* questions explore the meaning of the passage. *Application* questions help you discover the implications of the text for growing in Christ. These three keys unlock the treasures of Scripture.

Write your answers to the questions in the spaces provided or in a personal journal. Writing can bring clarity and deeper understanding of yourself and of God's Word.

5. It might be good to have a Bible dictionary handy. Use it to look up any unfamiliar words, names or places.

6. Use the prayer suggestion to guide you in thanking God for what you have learned and to pray about the applications that have come to mind.

7. You may want to go on to the suggestion under "Now or Later," or you may want to use that idea for your next study.

Suggestions for Members of a Group Study

1. Come to the study prepared. Follow the suggestions for individual study mentioned above. You will find that careful preparation will greatly enrich your time spent in group discussion.

2. Be willing to participate in the discussion. The leader of your group will not be lecturing. Instead, he or she will be encouraging the members of the group to discuss what they have learned. The leader will be asking the questions that are found in this guide.

3. Stick to the topic being discussed. Your answers should be based on the verses which are the focus of the discussion and not on outside authorities such as commentaries or speakers. These studies focus on a particular passage of Scripture. Only rarely should you refer to other portions of the Bible. This allows for everyone to participate in in-depth study on equal ground.

4. Be sensitive to the other members of the group. Listen attentively when they describe what they have learned. You may be surprised by their insights! Each question assumes a variety of answers. Many questions do not have "right" answers, particularly questions that aim at meaning or application. Instead, the questions push us to explore the passage more thoroughly.

When possible, link what you say to the comments of others. Also, be affirming whenever you can. This will encourage some of the more hesitant members of the group to participate.

5. Be careful not to dominate the discussion. We are sometimes so eager to express our thoughts that we leave too little opportunity for others to respond. By all means participate! But allow others to do so also.

6. Expect God to teach you through the passage being discussed and through the other members of the group. Pray that you will have an enjoyable and profitable time together, but also that as a result of the study you will find ways that you can take action individually or as a group.

7. If you are the group leader, you will find additional suggestions at the back of the guide.

1

A Holy God

Exodus 19:1 – 20:21

Why do we need to be forgiven — can't a God of love just accept us as we are? To go deeper in understanding forgiveness, we need first to appreciate more of our fundamental need of it. We often talk of God being holy, but holiness is a difficult concept to grasp in our age of relativism; yet this is a vital aspect of God's character.

To be holy has two shades of meaning: to be set apart or consecrated; and to have absolute moral purity.

GROUP DISCUSSION. What are some of the ways in which people — Christian and non-Christian — try to deal with guilt?

PERSONAL REFLECTION. What does guilt feel like to you?

In these chapters of Exodus, God gives an awesome, technicolour mega-display of what holiness is all about. He initiates an intensely significant meeting with his people, where he wants to lay the groundwork for their future relationship. *Read Exodus 19:1 – 20:21.*

1. What did the people have to do to prepare to meet with God (19:10–15)?

2. What was God seeking to communicate in giving these instructions to the people?

3. What happened when God came down onto the mountain (19:16–19)?

4. Try to imagine being there. What might you be thinking and feeling:

About God?

About yourself?

5. What implications could these thoughts and feelings have for your relationship with God in the future? (See also 20:20.)

6. Even though the Israelites had done all that was asked of them, how did they respond to this display of God's holiness (19:16; 20:18–21)?

7. Why do you think they responded in that way?

8. Why did Moses feel confident enough to approach God (19:20)?

Heb 4:15-16

_____

9. Which of the Ten Commandments (20:2–17) do you find hardest to keep?

_____

10. What are the consequences of failing to keep it in terms of:

Is 59:2

Your relationship with God?

Your relationship with others?

How you view yourself?

_____

11. What should be our motivation in trying to be obedient to God's commands (20:20)?   *Lev 19:2   Jn 14:21*

Spend some moments praying over these motivations. Ask God to help you remember them this week, whenever you are tempted to sin.

Now or Later

Read Isaiah 6:1–8. Isaiah had a vision of the holiness of God. What can you learn from his response to this vision?

2

We Need an Intermediary

Hebrews 4:14–16; 7:23–27;

9:11–14,22; 10:10

If we wanted to be received by the Queen, most of us would need someone to be a go-between. We could not just saunter up to Buckingham Palace and expect to be allowed in. Despite the recent efforts of the Royal Family to be approachable, there is no easy access between ordinary citizens and royalty. Between sinful people and a holy God, the gulf is of inexpressible dimensions.

GROUP DISCUSSION. Think about different people who act as go-betweens for us — solicitors, estate agents, secretaries, etc. What sort of qualities do you look for in a go-between?

PERSONAL REFLECTION. How do you feel about coming into God's presence?

In the Old Testament book of Leviticus, we read how God established the system of priests and sacrifices to begin to bridge the gulf between him and his sinful people. This gave a picture of the infinitely greater priest (go-between) who was to come. The letter to the Hebrews was written to explain how the old priestly system and the new High Priest fitted together. *Read Hebrews 4:14–16; 7:23–27; 9:11–14,22; 10:10.*

1. How is Jesus, our high priest, described in these verses (4:14–15; 7:24–26)?

_____

2. What qualifies him to be our high priest?

_____

3. In what ways is he different from the priests of the Old Testament (7:27–28)?

_____

4. In what ways does his sacrifice differ from theirs (9:11–14)?

_____

5. Describe how you might feel if you were an Israelite following the old system of sacrifices.

_____

6. What did Jesus' sacrifice obtain for us (9:22; 10:10)?

Take some time to meditate on these truths, asking God to give you new insights as to their meaning. Praise and thank him for all he has done.

_____

7. Read Hebrews 10:10. What difference does it make to you that you are "made holy." in terms of how you view:

God?

Yourself?

Other Christians?

_____

8. What are we encouraged to do in Hebrews 4:14,16?

_____

9. Why are these things important?

What will be the result if we don't do these things?

How can you apply this to your life?

Prayerfully read through one of the Gospel accounts of the crucifixion. Express your thanks to Jesus for being willing to be your great high priest.

Now or Later

Read Isaiah 52:13 – 53:12. Think about the suffering Jesus endured and then the rewards he experienced as a result. Turn these thoughts into praise.

3

God is Merciful to a Serial Sinner

2 Samuel 11:1 – 12:25; Psalm 51

People often fear that God is keeping a record of what they have done wrong and that they will have to face it all on Judgement Day. They hope their good deeds will be enough to balance out the bad stuff. Is this really how God operates?

GROUP DISCUSSION. Think about some events in public life where people have refused to admit their wrongdoing until forced to do so by the media or the law courts. What effect did the eventual disclosure have on them and others' opinions of them?

PERSONAL REFLECTION. Why do we find it so hard to admit we have done wrong?

In some perverse way, it is encouraging to realise that one of God's most well-known servants, David, was also capable of the most blatant and heinous crimes. From what we know of his life, it is clear that he experienced heights of elation, demonstrated humility and incredible faith, but also sank to the depths in his relationship with God. This is a story of deception, conviction and restoration, from which God's mercy and holiness blaze out in equal measure. *Read 2 Samuel 11:1 – 12:25; Psalm 51.*

1. Which of God's commandments did David break (2 Samuel 11:1–27)?

How did he progress from one to the other?

At which points could he have stopped this progression?

Why didn't he just own up?

---

2. What was God's motivation in sending Nathan to David (2 Samuel 12:1–25)?

---

3. Why do you think Nathan used this storytelling technique to confront David?

---

4. What should have been the just punishment for these sins (12:5–6)?

---

5. What consequences of these sins did Nathan announce to David (2 Samuel 12:10–12,14)?

---

6. What responses could David have made when Nathan confronted him?

How do you respond when someone points out your sins?

---

7. In Psalm 51 on what basis did David ask for forgiveness (v. 1)?

---

8. He used words like "blot out, wash away, cleanse me ... and I shall be clean, wash me ... whiter than snow, save me." What pictures do these words give as to how God deals with our sin?

---

9. How do you think David felt when Nathan said, "The Lord has taken away your sin" (2 Samuel 12:13, Psalm 51:3,8)?

---

10. How do you think David's experience of God was changed by this encounter (Psalm 51:8,12,13,15,17)?

---

11. What can we learn from this incident about God's forgiveness and the reality of facing the consequences of sin in our daily lives?

"He who conceals his sins does not prosper, but whoever confesses and renounces them finds mercy" (Proverbs 28:13). *Take some time to thank God for his mercy. Ask for his help to be quick to confess and not to conceal sin.*

Now or Later

Think about how you can go on believing you are forgiven, even when the memories of the sin keep coming back into your mind. Talk with Christian friends if you need help with this.

4

Jesus as Defence Lawyer

John 8:1–11

"I'll never rob anyone ever again. I've learned my lesson." I've heard these words many times from prisoners about to be released from jail. Whatever we may think about the justice system, prison is meant to be a deterrent to future law-breaking; the hope is that, having served their term, ex-prisoners will live exemplary lives. Unfortunately, statistics do not indicate that this happens in reality.

GROUP DISCUSSION. What do you find helps you to overcome sinful patterns of behaviour? Can we just blithely go on sinning and expect God to do the decent thing and forgive us?

PERSONAL REFLECTION. Think of one of your habitual sins. Are you making progress in overcoming this?

In any courtroom drama on TV, the defendant often takes a passive role. The battle takes place between the prosecution and defence lawyers. What the defendant needs, whether innocent or guilty, is an experienced lawyer on his side, who can represent his interests rightly and get the best possible outcome from the trial. In this incident, Jesus is drawn in to play the role of the defence lawyer, with surprising results. *Read John 8:1–11.*

1. Imagine the scene, using your senses. Listen to the noise of the crowd, smell the aromas, feel the tension. Then consider each group: the teachers of the law and the Pharisees; the woman; Jesus; the crowd. What might each group be doing and feeling? Think about the expressions on their faces.

2. What was the punishment for adultery (v. 5)?

3. ·Why did the teachers of the law bring only the woman (v. 6)?

4. How might the woman have felt about being accused in this way?

5. If Jesus had said, "OK, stone her," what could have happened?

6. If Jesus had said, "No, let her off," what could have happened?

7. Why did the men all go away?

8. Why didn't the woman run away?

9. What can we learn from her about how to respond when we are confronted with our sin?

10. What qualities did Jesus demonstrate throughout this encounter?

11. What do you think was in the woman's mind as she left?

12. Is there an area in your life where you need to make some changes?

Take some moments to thank Jesus for being your defence lawyer. "But if anybody does sin, we have one who speaks to the Father in our defence — Jesus Christ, the Righteous One. He is the atoning sacrifice for our sins, and not only for ours but also for the sins of the whole world" (1 John 2:1–2).

Now or Later

Read Colossians 3:5–14. Is there some attitude, action or thought which you need to "take off" so that you can increasingly grow into the new creature you have become in Christ? Make this a matter of daily prayer and ask others to pray for you. If you write a journal, make notes of your progress. If you don't already keep a journal, why not have a go at starting one? Write down your thoughts and feelings about what God is showing you.

5

God Forgives Exuberantly

Luke 15:11–32

Six-year-old Laura glared angrily at her younger brother and then at her headless Barbie doll. "Sorry, Laura," he whimpered. "I didn't mean it." Laura knew she had to forgive him, but she was going to make him suffer! The words she uttered, "OK, I forgive you," were in marked contrast to the menace in her eyes! They said, "You wait until Mum goes out, then I'll get you!"

GROUP DISCUSSION. Describe a recent example when you forgave someone. What was your attitude? What were you thinking about them?

PERSONAL REFLECTION. Think also about when you recently asked for forgiveness. How did the person respond to you? What do you think was going on in their minds and emotions?

What do you think is the expression on God's face when a person comes to him to confess their sin? Stern, disapproving, kind, exasperated? Jesus tells three parables — the lost sheep, the lost coin, the lost son — in rapid succession. It is as though he is using a megaphone to shout, "This is the way your Father forgives you!!" Read about the lost son, *Luke 15:11–32*.

1. What attitudes did the younger son display towards his father (vv. 11–13)?

_____

2. When he began to be in need, what choices did he have?

_____

3. When we begin to be aware of our own sin, what choices do we have?

_____

4. How was the son expecting to be received by his father (vv. 18–19)?

_____

5. How do you expect God to receive you when you come to him and confess your sin? What images of him do you have in your mind?

_____

6. What does the phrase "I am no longer worthy to be called your son" indicate about the son's understanding of his position in the household (v. 19)?

_____

7. What is the basis of a believer's position in God's household?

_____

8. What attitudes did the father display towards his returning son (vv. 20,22–24,32)?

9. What risk did the father take when he welcomed his son home again?

10. In verses 28–30, what attitudes did the older brother display towards:

His father?

His younger brother?

11. Think of recent times when you sinned. Was your concept of God more like the father or the older brother?

12. Describe ways that have helped you grow in understanding God's joy in forgiving his children. How can you deepen this understanding?

Ask God to help you dispel negative images of him from your mind and replace them with the truths you have discovered from this study.

Now or Later

Read through the other parables in Luke chapter 15 — the lost sheep (vv. 1–7) and the lost coin (vv. 8–10). What attitudes are displayed by the shepherd and the woman in their search for what was lost and when they find what they are seeking? Turn these thoughts into praise and thanks to God.

6

Greater Love for God

Luke 7:36–50

Whenever I visit prisons, I hear loud protestations of the inmates' innocence. "I didn't do it! I'm not guilty!" We all prefer to hide our sins and failures, just as Adam and Eve hid from God in the garden when their disobedience had become apparent. The fantastic thing about the Christian gospel is that the more we face up to our sins and confess them, the more forgiveness we experience. This greater revelation of God's mercy then stimulates a deeper response of love in our hearts. There is always much more sin in our hearts than we will ever comprehend, but God's forgiveness also runs to unfathomable depths!

GROUP DISCUSSION. In what ways have you experienced God's love over the past few months?

PERSONAL REFLECTION. In what ways have you expressed your love to God over the past few months?

This passage reveals an interesting cross-section of humanity — Simon the Pharisee, Jesus, an unnamed prostitute and other guests. Jesus is being entertained to a meal at a rather genteel middle-class home. Gradually it becomes apparent that an embarrassing incident is occurring. *Read Luke 7:36–50.*

1. Why was each of them there on that particular day? What might have been going on in their minds?

_____

2. How might each of them have responded to the events of verses 37–38?

_____

3. Jesus is a master storyteller. What was the point in this story (vv. 41–42)?

_____

4. Was Jesus implying that the woman was a greater sinner than Simon?

_____

5. What was Simon's understanding of his own need of forgiveness (v. 39)?

_____

6. How did this affect his thoughts and actions (vv. 39,44–46)?

_____

7. What clues do you see in this passage about the woman's awareness of her sin?

_____

8. What did it cost her to express her love and gratitude in this way?

9. In what ways do you express your love and gratitude to God for forgiveness?

10. Blatant sin is easy to identify. How can we become more aware of the hidden sins in our hearts?

11. On what basis was the woman forgiven (v. 50)?

12. What can we learn from Jesus' words, "Your sins are forgiven" (v. 48) and "go in peace" (v. 50)?

Ask God to help you find new ways of expressing your love and gratitude to him for forgiveness.

Now or Later

Take some time to pray, using Psalm 139:23–24 and Psalm 19:12 as a basis for your prayers. Ask God to reveal any sin he wants you to be aware of at this time. Allow the seriousness of the sin to touch you.

Read 1 John 1:9. Confess fully, then allow God's forgiveness to flow through you. Praise him that your sins are forgiven and that you can "go in peace."

7

Forgive Others

Matthew 18:21–35

Can you remember this song?

Love and marriage, love and marriage,
Go together like a horse and carriage.
Dad was told by Mother,
"You can't have one without the other!"

The same applies to forgiveness. Jesus taught his disciples to pray,
"Forgive us our sins for we also forgive everyone who sins against us"
(Luke 11:4). We cannot accept God's forgiveness and then refuse to
forgive others. Nor can we forgive others without first knowing the joy
and release of being forgiven by God. You can't have one without the
other!

GROUP DISCUSSION. What are some of the greatest examples you can
think of, outside the Bible, of a person forgiving another?

PERSONAL REFLECTION. How might you have reacted in similar
circumstances?

Peter probably thought he was being very magnanimous when he
suggested he should forgive his sinning brother seven times. For some
of us even seven times seems too hard. Jesus puts this question in a
completely different dimension. *Read Matthew 18:21–35.*

1. What characteristics of forgiveness is Jesus illustrating through the actions of the king in this parable, in terms of extent, motivation, attitude?

Does the debtor deserve to be forgiven?

2. What point is Jesus making in using these two different amounts of debt?

3. How did the servant respond to this amazing gesture of grace (vv. 28–30)?

4. Did the forgiven servant need the money owed him by his fellow servant?

5. Would it have been easy for him to forgive this debt?

6. Why do people find it hard to forgive others?

7. How do the characteristics you found in Question 1 relate to the difficulties you expressed in Question 6?

_____

8. What does this parable teach about the consequences of not forgiving?

_____

9. In what ways can unwillingness to forgive be a "prison"?

_____

10. What things have you found helpful in dealing with your unwillingness to forgive in your own life?

"The Lord is full of compassion and mercy" (James 5:11). Spend some moments thanking God for his endless supply of compassion and mercy to cover your own sin and to enable you to forgive others.

Now or Later

Jesus said, "Father, forgive them for they do not know what they are doing" (Luke 23:34). Write down all the things Jesus had to forgive in others at this time. Then, alongside that list, write down what you are facing at present in terms of forgiving others. Jesus knows what it feels like to be sinned against. Ask for his help to begin expressing his forgiveness to those who have sinned against you.

8

Keep on Forgiving

Luke 17:1–6

Jesus' cry from the cross, "Father, forgive them for they do not know what they are doing," stands as a blazing beacon pouring light on our human condition. History reveals lack of forgiveness in world conflicts as well as desperate individual and family pain. Former Yugoslavia and Ireland are but two international battlegrounds founded on and fuelled by the inability to forgive. There are wrongs on both sides, and a spiralling descent into ever-increasing horror is inevitable unless someone says, "I forgive."

GROUP DISCUSSION. Are there limits to the forgiveness we should extend to people like Judas, Hitler, Pol Pot, Stalin, an abusive partner?

PERSONAL REFLECTION. What questions do you have in your mind about the command to "keep on forgiving"?

Jesus knew that his time with his disciples was drawing to a close and he had some important teaching to pass on to them. He started with, "Don't expect life to be easy." *Read Luke 17:1–6.*

1. What is Jesus communicating here about a realistic view of life (v. 1a)?

2. Does this differ from how you expect the Christian life to be?

3. What are some practical implications of Jesus' view of life?

4. What is our responsibility if we sin repeatedly?

5. How should we respond if we are repeatedly sinned against (v. 4)?

6. What difference does it make if the person does not repent?

7. How do Jesus' disciples respond to this teaching (v. 5)?

8. How do you respond to Jesus' teaching?

9. Summarise Jesus' response (v. 6).

10. What is the relationship between faith and forgiveness?

_____

11. What steps can you take to grow in faith in this context?

Lord, thank you for your amazing example of forgiveness to those who wronged you. Help me to become more like you in this area.

Now or Later

Review the last study, "Forgive Others," and this one, "Keep on Forgiving." Bring any situation of unforgiveness to God and ask him to help you take one step forward in the process of being able to forgive. It would be helpful to pray over this with a friend if you can.

9

Hold No Grudges

Genesis 45:1–15; 50:15–21

Joseph had been deeply wronged. He may well have been an irritating and spoilt brat, but the way his older brothers treated him was totally out of proportion to his misdemeanours. During his time in Egypt, he was not only accused but imprisoned for a crime he didn't commit; then he was forgotten by those whom he had helped. He had, humanly speaking, every reason to hold massive grudges against several people, and to want them to suffer for the way they had ill-treated him.

GROUP DISCUSSION. Describe some situations in real life or in books you've read, where people exacted revenge for wrongs committed against them.

PERSONAL REFLECTION. The old saying is, "Revenge is sweet." What is gained by taking revenge and what is lost by it?

We pick up the story of Joseph when he is a ruler in Egypt and his brothers have come to buy food because of the famine in the land. His brothers have not yet recognised him, probably because he was a young boy when they sold him as a slave and he is in a totally different context from what they could ever have expected. *Read Genesis 45:1–15; 50:15–21.*

1. From your knowledge of the ups and downs of Joseph's life, what would be some of the feelings he would have experienced over his years of suffering?

_____

2. In what ways can you identify with any of his feelings?

_____

3. When he makes himself known to his brothers, what is his attitude towards:

His brothers?

His father?

His whole extended family?

_____

4. What is Joseph's understanding of God's character and purposes (45:4–8; 50:20)?

_____

5. How do you think Joseph came to these conclusions about God?

_____

6. How did his brothers react to Joseph (45:3,14–15; 50:15–18)?

_____

7. What does their reaction reveal about them?

_____

8. If Joseph had wanted to exact revenge, what might have happened:

To him and his relationship with God?

To his brothers and his whole family?

_____

9. How has this study helped you in coping with injustice and hurt?

Ask God to help you let go of any grudges you are holding and release forgiveness to the offender.

Now or Later

Read the story of David, Nabal and Abigail, in 1 Samuel 25:1–42. What lessons can you learn about forgiveness and vengeance from this story?

10

Forgive Yourself

Matthew 27:1–10;

Luke 22:60–62;

John 21:15–17

What drives one man to suicide and enables another man to inspire many to serve God wholeheartedly, not only during his lifetime but for 2,000 years since? We've seen in the previous chapters how God has poured out his forgiveness on us and how he expects us to respond in love to him and in forgiveness towards others. Forgiving ourselves is a vital part of this process.

GROUP DISCUSSION. What happens to our relationship with God and with others when we don't forgive ourselves?

PERSONAL REFLECTION. Think of a recent situation where you found it hard to forgive yourself. Try to describe your thought processes.

We still carry the guilt

Judas and Peter were both specially chosen disciples of Jesus and had been with him for about three years. The outcome of their lives could not have been more different. One reason for this is their different understanding of forgiveness. We'll read their stories to glean insights to help us. *Read Matthew 27:1–10; Luke 22:60–62; John 21:15–17.*

1. What was Judas' understanding of his sin (Matthew 27:3–4)?

2. To whom did he confess his sin?

3. What do you think were his thoughts on leaving the chief priests?

Foolishnes
Dispair, Lonelines

4. In what ways can you identify with Judas' thoughts and feelings?

5. What choices did he have at this point?

He could have confessed to God
He chose to be alone
Too proud to confess

6. How did Peter respond after he became aware of his sin (Luke 22:60–62)?

7. Why do you think Jesus looked at Peter at that moment? What was conveyed in that look (v. 61)?

That Jesus knew His heart

8. How do you think Peter felt when Jesus looked at him?

9. From what you know of Peter's life, what choices did he make at this point?

He chose to be with friends

10. In what ways did Jesus help Peter to come to terms with what he had done (John 21:15–17)?

11. From this conversation, what convictions did Peter have which gave him confidence to come to Jesus?

He knew Jesus knew his heart
See Heb 4:13 "Nothing in all creation is hidden from God's sight"

12. How do you think Peter felt after this conversation with Jesus?

Able to receive His forgiveness

13. Summarise the principles you have discovered in these passages which promote a healthy forgiveness of oneself.

Ask God for his help to receive his forgiveness, to forgive others and to forgive yourself.

Now or Later

Take some time to reflect back over these studies. Pick out a few points, with relevant Bible verses, which have impressed you deeply. Write these out and share them with a friend. Ask God to help you take significant steps in these vital areas of forgiveness. Thank him for the cross which makes it all possible.

Leader's Notes

MY GRACE IS SUFFICIENT FOR YOU. (2 COR 12:9)

Leading a Bible discussion can be an enjoyable and rewarding experience. But it can also be *scary* — especially if you've never done it before. If this is your feeling, you're in good company. When God asked Moses to lead the Israelites out of Egypt, he replied, "O Lord, please send someone else to do it!" (Exodus 4:13). It was the same with Solomon, Jeremiah and Timothy, but God helped these people in spite of their weaknesses and he will help you as well.

You don't need to be an expert on the Bible or a trained teacher to lead a Bible discussion. The idea behind these inductive studies is that the leader guides group members to discover for themselves what the Bible has to say. This method of learning will allow group members to remember much more of what is said than a lecture would.

These studies are designed to be led easily. As a matter of fact, the flow of questions through the passage from observation to interpretation to application is so natural that you may feel that the studies lead themselves. This study guide is also flexible. You can use it with a variety of groups — student, professional, neighbourhood or church groups. Each study takes forty-five to sixty minutes in a group setting.

There are some important facts to know about group dynamics and encouraging discussion. The suggestions listed below should enable you to fulfil your role as leader effectively and enjoyably.

Preparing for the Study

1. Ask God to help you understand and apply the passage in your own life. Unless this happens, you will not be prepared to lead others. Pray too for the various members of the group. Ask God to open your hearts to the message of his Word and motivate you to action.

2. Read the introduction to the guide to get an overview of the entire book and the issues which will be explored.

3. As you begin each study, read and reread the assigned Bible passage to familiarise yourself with it.

4. This study guide is based on the New International Version of the Bible. It will help you and the group if you use this translation as the basis for your study and discussion.

5. Carefully work through each question in the study. Spend time in meditation and reflection as you consider how to respond.

6. Write your thoughts and responses in the space provided in the study guide. This will help you to express your understanding of the passage clearly.

7. It might help to have a Bible dictionary handy. Use it to look up any unfamiliar words, names or places. (For additional help on how to study a passage, see chapter five of *Leading Bible Discussions*, InterVarsity Press.)

8. Consider how you can apply the Scripture to your life. Remember that the group will follow your lead in responding to the studies. They will not go any deeper than you do.

9. Once you have finished your own study of the passage, familiarise yourself with the leader's notes for the study you are leading. These are designed to help you in several ways. First, they tell you the purpose the study guide author had in mind when writing the study. Take time to think through how the study questions work together to accomplish that purpose. Second, the notes provide you with additional background information or suggestions on group dynamics for various questions. This information can be useful when people have difficulty understanding or answering a question. Third, the leader's notes can alert you to potential problems you may encounter during the study.

10. If you wish to remind yourself of anything mentioned in the leader's notes, make a note to yourself below that question in the study.

Leading the Study

1. Begin the study on time. Open with prayer, asking God to help the group understand and apply the passage.

2. Be sure that everyone in your group has a study guide. Encourage the group to prepare beforehand for each discussion by reading the introduction to the guide and by working through the questions in the study.

3. At the beginning of your first session together, explain that these studies are meant to be discussions, not lectures. Encourage the members

of the group to participate. However, do not put pressure on those who may be hesitant to speak during the first few sessions. You may want to suggest the following guidelines to your group.

● Stick to the topic being discussed.

● Your responses should be based on the verses which are the focus of the discussion and not on outside authorities such as commentaries or speakers.

● These studies focus on a particular passage of Scripture. Only rarely should you refer to other portions of the Bible. This allows for everyone to participate in in-depth study on equal ground.

● Anything said in the group is considered confidential and will not be discussed outside the group unless specific permission is given to do so.

● We will listen attentively to each other and provide time for each person to talk.

● We will pray for each other.

4. Have a group member read the introduction at the beginning of the discussion.

5. Every session begins with a group discussion question. The question or activity is meant to be used before the passage is read. The question introduces the theme of the study and encourages group members to begin to open up. Encourage as many members as possible to participate and be ready to get the discussion going with your own response.

This section is designed to reveal where our thoughts or feelings need to be transformed by Scripture. That is why it is especially important not to read the passage before the discussion question is asked. The passage will tend to colour the honest reactions people would otherwise give because they are, of course, supposed to think the way the Bible does.

You may want to supplement the group discussion question with an ice-breaker to help people get comfortable. For ideas, see Appendix A in *The Small-Group Leader* by John Mallison (Scripture Union).

You also might want to use the "personal reflection" question with your group. Either allow a time of silence for people to respond individually or discuss it together.

6. Have a group member (or members, if the passage is long) read aloud the passage to be studied. Then give people several minutes to read the passage again silently so that they can take it all in.

7. Question 1 will generally be an overview question designed briefly

to survey the passage. Encourage the group to do this, but try to avoid getting sidetracked by questions or issues that will be addressed later in the study.

8. As you ask the questions, keep in mind that they are designed to be used just as they are written. You may simply read them aloud, or you may prefer to express them in your own words.

There may be times when it is appropriate to deviate from the study guide. For example, a question may already have been answered. If so, move on to the next. Or someone may raise an important question not covered in the guide. Take time to discuss it, but try to keep the group from going off at a tangent.

9. Avoid answering your own questions. If necessary, repeat or rephrase them until they are clearly understood, or point out something you read in the leader's notes to clarify context or meaning. An eager group quickly becomes passive and silent if they think the leader will do most of the talking.

10. Don't be afraid of silence. People may need time to think about the question before formulating their answer.

11. Don't be content with just one answer. Ask, "What do the rest of you think?" or "Anything else?" until several people have given answers to the question.

12. Acknowledge all contributions. Try to be affirming whenever possible. Never reject an answer. If it is clearly off-base, ask, "Which verse led you to that conclusion?" or again, "What do the rest of you think?"

13. Don't expect every answer to be addressed to you, even though this will probably happen at first. As group members become more at ease, they will begin to truly interact with each other. This is one sign of healthy discussion.

14. Don't be afraid of controversy. It can be very stimulating. If you don't resolve an issue completely, don't be frustrated. Move on and keep it in mind for later. A subsequent study may solve the problem.

15. Periodically, summarise what the group has said about the passage. This helps to draw together the various ideas mentioned and gives continuity to the study. But don't preach!

16. At the end of the Bible discussion, you may want to allow group members a time of quiet to work on an idea under "Now or Later." Then discuss what you experienced. Or you may want to encourage group members to work on these ideas between meetings. Give an opportunity

during the session to allow people to talk about what they are learning.

17. Conclude your time together with conversational prayer, adapting the prayer suggestion at the end of the study to your group. Ask for God's help in following through on the commitments you have made.

18. End on time.

Many more suggestions and helps are found in *Leading Bible Discussions* (InterVarsity Press).

Components of Small Groups

A healthy small group should do more than study the Bible. There are four components to consider as you structure your time together.

Nurture. Small groups help us to grow in our knowledge and love of God. Bible study is the key to making this happen and is the foundation of your small group.

Community. Small groups are a great place to develop deep friendships with other Christians. Allow time for informal interaction before and after each study. Plan activities and games that will help you to get to know each other. Spend time having fun together — going on a picnic or cooking dinner together.

Worship and prayer. Your study will be enhanced by spending time praising God together in prayer or song. Pray for each other's needs and keep track of how God is answering prayer in your group. Ask God to help you apply what you are learning in your study.

Outreach. Reaching out to others can be a practical way of applying what you are learning and it will keep your group from becoming self-focused. Host a series of evangelistic discussions for your friends or neighbours. Clean up the yard of an elderly friend. Serve at a soup kitchen together, or spend a day working on a Habitat house.

Many more suggestions and helps in each of these areas are found in *Small Group Idea Book* (InterVarsity Press). Other resources for establishing a small group are *Small Group Leaders' Handbook* and *The Big Book on Small Groups* (both from InterVarsity Press), and *The Small-Group Leader* and *Small Group Starter Kit* (both from Scripture Union).

Study 1. A Holy God. Exodus 19:1 – 20:21.

Purpose: To understand more of God's utter holiness and therefore our need of forgiveness so we can approach his holy throne. .

General note. Definition of holiness: "Holiness means ... separated or set apart for God and his service, thus ... holy ground (Ex.3:5), holy assembly (12:16), holy Sabbath (16:23), holy nation (19:6) and holy place (29:31) ... Similarly, God sanctified the people of Israel by separating them from all the nations of the earth ... but this involved giving to them a knowledge of the divine law, moral and ceremonial. Thus the ethical is imparted. These two aspects of holiness are generally present, since it was understood that being holy meant not only living a separate life, but bearing a character different from that of the ordinary man" (*The Illustrated Bible Dictionary*, InterVarsity Press).

Group discussion. If group members don't know one another very well, it would be important to be sensitive to those who may not feel able to share personally on this subject. The question is phrased generally, not subjectively.

Question 1. This is a *discovery* question. Try not to get bogged down with discussion about it — just get a list of what is required.

Question 2. This is an *understanding* question. In studying the Scriptures, it is important to see first what the passage says before trying to understand what it means. Holiness is a difficult concept to grasp because of our ease of access to God through Jesus. In Old Testament times, the Jews would have known they needed to approach God with reverential fear, having first covered their sin by washing and sacrifices.

Question 4. It might be helpful to get people to close their eyes. Then read verses 16–19 again fairly slowly to enable people to imagine themselves into the situation. Suggest they use their five senses — sight, hearing, smell, touch, speech. Don't rush this question.

Question 8. Moses was invited by God to approach him. Through the sacrifice of Jesus, we also now have that privilege (Hebrews 4:15–16).

Question 10. It is important that we grasp the awfulness and consequences of sin so that we can grow in understanding Christ's magnificent gift of forgiveness. Allow people the time to explore these questions fully. Isaiah 59:2 is a helpful cross-reference.

Question 11. Leviticus 19:2 and John 14:21 will give additional insights to this question.

At the end of the study, encourage the group to ask God to teach them more about his holiness in the intervening weeks. However, stress the need to keep praising and thanking God for his wonderful gift of forgiveness.

Study 2. We Need an Intermediary. Hebrews 4:14–16; 9:11–14,22; 10:10.

Purpose: To see that Jesus is the believer's perfect high priest, having paid the full price for our forgiveness.

General note. It would be helpful to ask people what they remembered from the previous study on God's holiness, as this will pave the way for a greater understanding of our need of a high priest.

If any of your group members have little knowledge of the Old Testament, it would be good to read all the passages relating to this study first. You may need to explain that God wanted to emphasise his holiness to his people and show them that their sin caused a separation. The system of priest and sacrifices were God's way of making it possible for there to be a relationship between God and man. But this system was a symbol of the far greater and utterly sufficient sacrifice that Jesus offered.

Questions 1–4. These are *discovery* questions. It is important to get all the facts out into the open. You may find it helpful to have a blackboard or a large sheet of paper and to invite one of the group to write out the answers given to Questions 3 and 4, making two lists to enable a comparison between Jesus and the Old Testament priests and their offerings.

If you add to that list the answers to Question 6 — What did his sacrifice obtain for us? — this will make it easier for people to meditate on these truths and to begin to appreciate more fully the difference Jesus has made to us.

Question 7. The NIV Study Bible notes on 1 Corinthians 1:2 are helpful here: "made holy" is done by (1) being declared holy through faith in Christ's atoning death on the cross (sometimes called positional sanctification), and (2) being made holy by the work of the Holy Spirit in the lives of Christians (sometimes called progressive sanctification). In spite of the fact that Paul found much in the Corinthian Christians to criticise, he still called them "sanctified" — not because of their conduct, but because of their relationship to Christ (positional sanctification). So, being "made holy" is something which has already happened to believers because of their relationship with Christ, though they are also growing into that status by the work of the Holy Spirit within them.

Question 8. Satan often attacks believers in this area of forgiveness, tempting them to doubt God's word. They feel guilty and condemned. Satan means "accuser" (Revelation 12:10). Hebrews 4:14 urges us to "hold firmly to the faith we profess." For those in your group who have a particular struggle with guilt, it is vital that they hold on to the truth of God's word. Memorising a verse can be a life-saver — the Holy Spirit can bring it to mind when Satan comes in with his accusations. You could suggest that as a group you learn a relevant verse and encourage one another in that way. In the following study time, you could check each other on whether you have learned it and how it has been helpful to you in the intervening time.

Prayer suggestion. You could suggest that people close their eyes. Then read an account of the crucifixion using a different version of the Bible, e.g. *The Message*, a paraphrase by Eugene Peterson, so that the passage comes across with freshness. You might like to end by sharing thoughts, or with prayer and praise, either singing or listening to a tape of a hymn or a chorus focusing on the cross.

Study 3. God is Merciful to a Serial Sinner. 2 Samuel 11:1 – 12:25; Psalm 51.

Purpose: To understand that God's immense mercy can cover the most awful sins. But to receive it we need to be honest and up-front with him about what we have done wrong.

General note. It would be good at the beginning to ascertain if everyone in the group understands who King David was. To avoid embarrassing people, you could prime a couple of group members who would be willing and able to give a quick résumé of David's life up to this point of his adultery with Bathsheba. It is helpful to realise that even after years of walking with God one is not immune from temptation and eventual sin. See 1 Corinthians 10:11–13.

Question 1. As this is a fairly long reading, it would be good to get the group to look for the answers to this question while the passage is being read. This will help to focus their attention.

Question 2. God's motivation in rebuking his children is to restore them to fellowship with him, not to condemn and make them feel awful. See Galatians 6:1. Note that a believer's *relationship* with God is not in doubt here, but the enjoyment of that relationship, *fellowship*, is hindered by sin.

Question 3. David basically condemned himself by his response to this story. The important point in our walk with God is not so much that we sin, but that we own up to it quickly. See Proverbs 28:13.

Question 4. See also Leviticus 20:10; Deuteronomy 22:22.

Question 7. David pleaded for forgiveness on the basis of God's love and compassion. As believers on this side of the cross, we too can ask for mercy on the basis of Christ's death for us. It would be good to stress that our forgiveness was bought at an incredibly high price and that sin, therefore, should never be trivialised. God is holy as well as merciful. Note that David made no reference to his past good deeds or tried to justify himself in any way. Ephesians 2:8–9 states clearly that we are saved by grace alone, not by any works.

Question 10. This is an important question for those who find it hard to feel forgiven. David knew that God did not want him to live with guilt, so he asked for joy and renewed opportunities to teach others God's ways. He embraced full forgiveness.

Question 11. God forgives the guilt of our sin and restores our fellowship with him, but he will not obliterate the consequences of our sinful actions. For example, if we choose an unhealthy lifestyle and abuse our body in some way, we will be forgiven if we repent but we may experience ill-health. However, God, in his wisdom and compassion, can use these consequences for good in our lives. See Romans 8:28; Hebrews 12:5–11.

Study 4. Jesus as Defence Lawyer. John 8:1–11.

Purpose: To grow in understanding that Jesus is our Defender, not our Accuser, and that a change in lifestyle should follow our experience of forgiveness.

Question 1. It would be helpful to invite the group to close their eyes. Then read the verses slowly, using more than one translation.

Question 2. The NIV Study Bible states that whereas the teachers of the law said that Moses commanded the stoning of such women, "...they altered the law a little. The manner of execution was not prescribed unless the woman was a betrothed virgin (Deuteronomy 22:23–24). And the law required the execution of both parties (Leviticus 20:10; Deuteronomy 22:22), not just the woman."

Questions 5–6. It is clear that the teachers of the law were using this woman as a pretext to entrap Jesus. To condemn her to stoning would have brought Jesus into conflict with the Roman authorities, as Jews were not allowed to inflict the death penalty. To condone her sin would demonstrate that Jesus disregarded the law God gave through Moses. This would have given the teachers of the law justification to silence Jesus and would also have lost him the sympathy of the crowd.

General note. It is probably not helpful to speculate about what Jesus wrote on the ground. One side effect of this could have been that it took the attention away from the woman, as people would have been intrigued about what he was writing. She would have been very grateful that people were not staring at her.

Question 8. Something in Jesus' attitude must have shown the woman that it was better to stay than to run and hide. In staying there, she was facing up to her sin and was therefore able to receive forgiveness. Note that she did not blame the teachers of the law, even though she had clearly been "set-up," nor did she protest her innocence or rationalise her guilt.

Question 10. In this encounter, Jesus displayed compassion and fairness to all involved. He did not take sides or accuse. The teachers of the law thought they had the situation totally in hand, but Jesus' wisdom triumphed over all their machinations.

Question 11. An important point to bring out here is that Jesus said, "Go now and leave your life of sin." A change in lifestyle was demanded.

Study 5. God Forgives Exuberantly. Luke 15:11–32.

Purpose: To understand that God delights to forgive sinners, and that his forgiveness is complete, freely given and fully restores our fellowship with him (see Micah 7:18).

Question 1. Some attitudes were: greed, not caring about his father's needs, disloyalty, arrogance and contempt for all his father's hard work.

Question 3. Our choices are to ignore it or to repent of it. To ignore sin in our lives will inevitably lead to deeper involvement in sin (Romans 1:22–23,32). The Christian life is never static — we are either growing to be more like Jesus (2 Corinthians 3:18) or growing further from him. The phrase "when he came to his senses" in verse 17 is interesting to note. When he faced the situation squarely, he was able to make rational choices. The most sensible thing was to return home to his father. The only thing he would lose was his pride. To allow anything to keep us from dealing with sin is utterly counter-productive. We need to come to our senses and deal with it as quickly as possible.

Question 5. Some images in people's minds could be related to their experience of their human parents, e.g. stern disciplinarian, doting parent, distant emotional relationship. They may not want to make the connection during the group time, but might appreciate talking this through with you or another trusted friend. It would be good to be available to your group members if they wanted to talk more privately.

Questions 6–7. The important point to bring out here is that none of us is worthy. This is not the basis on which we approach God or are members of his household — it is all by grace (Ephesians 2:8,9).

Question 9. The risk is that the son would again abuse his kindness. This is also the risk that God takes when he showers his love and mercy on us.

Question 12. It is vital to focus on the truth. Micah 7:18 says that God delights "to show mercy." Meditating and learning verses will help. You can also use your imagination. Picture yourself being welcomed back into God's loving arms. Think of the fantastic smile on his face!

Study 6. Greater Love for God. Luke 7:36–50.

Purpose: To understand that our love for God will grow as we face up to sin in our lives and experience more of his forgiveness.

General note. As you start this second section, it would be helpful to do a quick résumé of the first five studies. Just say a sentence or two about each so that the truths about the forgiving nature of God are firmly in people's minds as they focus on how they will respond.

It is important also to be aware that some people have a more sensitive conscience than others and more quickly feel condemned and unworthy when convicted of sin. Others need to take sin more seriously so that they appreciate more fully what they have been delivered from.

Sin and forgiveness are sensitive subjects and need careful handling. Pray for God to give you wisdom to know what aspects to emphasise in your group.

Question 1. This story may well be very familiar to some of the group. This question is aimed at helping them take a fresh look at it. The woman didn't just turn up at the meal. She had no doubt heard Jesus preach and had repented. She was overwhelmed with love and gratitude and wanted somehow to express it. Jesus was relaxed and comfortable, even though it was a potentially embarrassing situation.

Question 3. Some Christians get discouraged when they become more conscious of sin. They feel as if they are regressing. However, in reality it is usually a sign of growth. God only shows us a tiny part of our sin, otherwise we would be completely devastated by the awfulness of it. But the more we see, the more we need to fully embrace his forgiveness.

Question 4. Romans 3:23 clearly teaches that we have all fallen short of God's standard.

Question 8. The costs to this woman were the price of the perfume and the courage it took to go to a place where she knew she would not be welcome. Keep these thoughts in mind as you discuss Question 9.

Question 9. Apart from an emphasis on praise, worship and seeking to live a holy life, we can also show our love for God by loving others. Love is costly in terms of time, money, and emotional and physical energy.

Question 10. Psalm 139:23–24 and Psalm 19:12 give helpful insights.

Question 11. It is important to stress that the woman was forgiven on the basis of her faith, not on her showing love to Jesus (this would be earned forgiveness). "Love is the proof of the reception of forgiveness, and the more a person is forgiven, the more he will love" (New Bible Commentary).

Question 12. A common difficulty in this area of forgiveness is that we start well and believe we are forgiven, but then doubts creep in, especially when we are conscious of our failings and sin. This woman needed to believe Jesus' statement, "Your sins are forgiven" and to keep believing it so that she could "go in peace."

You could suggest that your group members choose a verse to meditate on and memorise, so that they have an anchor to keep them grounded in the truth when doubts come in.

Study 7. Forgive Others. Matthew 18:21–35.

Purpose: To understand that forgiving others is an indispensable part of being forgiven.

General note. Some of your group may have been so badly hurt by others that they feel unable to even begin to forgive. This could be a difficult study for them to cope with. Encourage them nevertheless to listen to God through the study. He is concerned that they make progress, however far back they feel. But it is important not to trivialise their experience.

Interpreting parables. There is usually one main point being made in a parable, and it is vital not to look for spiritual significance in every detail.

Question 2. Jesus deliberately uses a massive contrast — millions of pounds and a few pounds of debt — to illustrate the unbelievably huge measure of divine forgiveness that God has extended to us. Even though the wrongs committed against us may seem unbearable, we have already received forgiveness for far greater sins we have committed.

Questions 5–6. Forgiveness never is easy and it will cost us dearly, but not to forgive will cost much more in terms of pain in our relationship with God and others. If bitterness is allowed to take root, it will contaminate relationships all round (Hebrews 12:15). See also note on Question 9.

Question 8. It is important not to press the details, i.e. about the man being handed over to the jailers to be tortured. The New Bible Commentary says, "…not all the details of the parable are to be pressed. But the point is clear that the unforgiving man cannot be in a position of forgiveness before God. The man, forgiven by God through what Christ has done, will give in his treatment of others unmistakable evidence of his gratitude to and dependence upon him."

Question 9. Lewis Smedes points out in *Shame and Grace* (Triangle/SPCK): "When we genuinely forgive, we set a prisoner free and then discover that the prisoner we set free was us."

Question 10. For those in your group who are struggling with this issue, encourage them to be honest with God about how they feel. A first step is to pray to be willing to forgive, asking for God's help. Some people find it helpful to make a practical symbolic action, e.g. write out the problem and then burn the paper, symbolising that it has been dealt with. For those further along in the forgiving process, you can suggest that they pray for the one who wronged them and ask God to bless him or her (see Luke 6:45). This often releases power to forgive.

It is important after studying a topic like this to end by focusing on God's compassion and mercy. Perhaps the group could pray specifically for those who are struggling with this at the moment.

Study 8. Keep on Forgiving. Luke 17:1–6.

Purpose: To build on study 7 and understand that the forgiveness we offer to others should be unlimited.

General note. This again could be a difficult chapter for some of your group members. Encourage them to keep their hearts open to God and to trust him for help and healing. Ask God to give you wisdom as you lead your group through these difficult areas of life.

Question 1. Jesus' view of life was that trouble will come. We live in a fallen world and we cannot expect any human relationship to be easy or straightforward.

Question 2. In your group you may have optimists and pessimists who will view life differently. It is important to listen to all opinions and bring them back to Jesus' teaching. Realistically, we will sin against others and cause them harm, and others will sin against us and cause us harm.

Question 3. It would be good to invite the group to think about how they could be better prepared to face and resolve conflicts. There are resources available, i.e. books and tapes, which offer principles and guidance in these areas. For those who have children, how could they help them in this area?

Question 4. Matthew 5:23–24 is helpful here.

Question 5. In biblical tradition, the number seven is symbolic of completeness. Jesus is teaching that forgiveness should be unlimited. In his Tyndale New Testament Commentary on Matthew, R T France states: "Jesus' reply does away with all limits and calculations. His allusion to Genesis 4:24 neatly contrasts Lamech's unlimited vindictiveness with the unlimited forgiveness of the disciple. The Hebrew of Genesis 4:24 clearly means seventy-seven times ... but to be concerned as to whether the figure is 77 or 490 is to return to the pedantic calculation which Jesus rejects!"

Question 6. If the person does not repent, we still have a responsibility to forgive them, but the relationship with that person will be strained. "If it is possible, as far as it depends on you, live at peace with everyone" (Romans 12:18). From our side, there should be forgiveness offered, but we obviously cannot force someone to admit their guilt and repent of it. But if we do not forgive, we will be disobeying God and trapped in a cycle of resentment and bitterness (Hebrews 12:15).

Question 7. It is encouraging to note that the disciples felt completely inadequate when faced with this challenge. In effect they are saying, "We can't do it!"

Questions 9–10. Jesus says, in effect, "You have the faith — use it." Faith to believe God will forgive you, that he will enable you to forgive others, that he will heal the hurt and bring about justice in his way, in his time.

Question 11. Our faith needs to be based solidly on God's word. "Faith comes from hearing the message, and the message is heard through the word of Christ" (Romans 10:17). We need to take hold of God's commandments and his promises and go forward, not waiting for our feelings to prompt us into action. Praying with others is a real stimulus to faith, also recognising that it is a battle and will not be easy — but God's grace is sufficient (2 Corinthians 12:9).

Study 9. Hold No Grudges. Genesis 45:1–15; 50:15–21.

Purpose: To gain God's perspective on wrongs committed against us and therefore be enabled to let go of grudges and the desire for revenge.

General note. It would be good to give brief details of Joseph's life story as a reminder to those who might have forgotten and so as not to embarrass those who have not read about him. The full account of his life is found in Genesis chapters 37, 39–50.

Question 1. He would have felt the injustice of it ("It's not fair"); abandoned by God and his nearest and dearest; not in control of his life or decisions; anger, resentment, loneliness, fear (what else might go wrong?!).

Question 2. If your group has worked through the whole book together, they may well be willing to share honestly about their struggles at this point. Give opportunity for those who want to share, but don't put pressure on people to reveal their deepest secrets in a group context.

Question 3. Some important words are: "he wept" (v. 2), "come close" (v. 4), "the one you sold into Egypt" (v. 4); he did not deny his brothers' sinful actions — he "spoke the truth in love" (Ephesians 4:15); "do not be distressed or angry with yourselves" (v. 5), "hurry back", "come down" (v. 9)," you shall … be near me" (v. 10), "I will provide for you" (v. 11); he threw his arms around Benjamin; he wept, embraced and kissed them (vv. 14–15).

Question 4. He recognised God's sovereign control of his life and that God always had good purposes in mind — to save his people. He saw that God was faithful in working out his plan. He acknowledged that God alone had the right to judge. A key verse is Genesis 50:19, where Joseph asks his brothers, "Am I in the place of God?" Joseph saw himself as God's servant. When we want revenge, we are usurping God's place — we should "leave room for God's wrath" (Romans 12:19).

Question 5. Mostly we learn our lessons about God through suffering (James 1:2–4). Through the long years of waiting for God to rescue him, Joseph had the choice of trusting him or resisting him.

Joseph had certainly received teaching about God from his parents, Jacob and Rachel. Those experiences and the dreams that he had were no doubt anchors for him in the dark times. Similarly, when we go through difficult times, we should remember the ways God has helped us in the past. We can also anchor our faith on God's promises in his Word.

Question 7. The brothers' reaction of fear revealed the guilt in their hearts. They had never confessed or dealt with the sin they had committed, and it had festered in their hearts for years.

General note. In this whole area about revenge and the desire for justice, a passage from Philip Yancey's book, *What's So Amazing About Grace?*, is very helpful:

"Do not take revenge, my friends, but leave room for God's wrath, for it is written: 'It is mine to avenge; I will repay,' says the Lord"(Romans 12:19).

At last I understood: in the final analysis, forgiveness is an act of faith. By forgiving another I am trusting that God is a better justice-maker than I am. By forgiving, I release my own right to get even and leave all issues of fairness for God to work out. I leave in God's hands the scales that must balance justice and mercy.

When Joseph finally came to the place of forgiving his brothers, the hurt did not disappear, but the burden of being their judge fell away. Though wrong does not disappear when I forgive, it loses its grip on me and is taken over by God who knows what to do. Such a decision involves risk, of course, the risk that God may not deal with the person as I would want.

Study 10. Forgive Yourself. Matthew 27:1–10; Luke 22:60–62; John 21:15–17.

Purpose: To understand the reasons people don't forgive themselves, the consequences of not forgiving oneself, and some principles on how to forgive oneself.

Group discussion. If you don't forgive yourself, you still carry the guilt of the wrongdoing. This hinders intimacy with God and with others. You may feel unworthy to approach God. You may feel weary because of the emotional toll this takes. This would all have knock-on effects in terms of general well-being, witness, worship, etc.

Personal reflection. The main reasons are an inadequate grasp of God's grace and forgiveness, and being too proud to accept the reality of being a needy sinner. In some perverse way, we run away from the very thing that would free us. By not forgiving ourselves, we are saying that our standards of acceptability are higher than God's!

General note. It would be good to read all the passages in the first instance, then to go back and re-read the relevant passages as they apply to different questions. For those with very limited Bible knowledge, it would be helpful to outline briefly the lives of Judas and Peter.

Question 3. No doubt he felt a complete failure. Maybe other sins from the past came into his mind. His clever plan had failed. He must have felt foolish. The future must have looked very black indeed.

Question 5. He could have chosen to confess his sin to God, then find the other disciples and confess it to them, asking for their help. This would have been very humbling for him. But he chose to be alone and give in to despair.

Question 7. Some important points to bring out here are that Jesus would not have wanted Peter to fall into despair. Possibly in looking at him Jesus wanted to remind Peter of the warning he had given him — that he would deny him three times — thereby indicating that nothing Peter had done had shocked Jesus. In the same way, God is not surprised when we sin. He has total knowledge of our failures and mistakes, and has already provided the grace and forgiveness for us. In that look there must have been compassion, a desire to inspire hope, as well as sadness for the sin.

Question 9. Peter wept bitterly, then chose to be with his friends. He must have talked with them about what happened. He humbled himself before his friends and before God.

Question 10. Jesus took Peter through a three-fold commitment and gave him a new responsibility. The three denials were counteracted by three declarations of love.

Question 11. Peter states that Jesus knew everything about him, even his innermost thoughts. When we realise that we don't have to pretend to God or anyone else, even ourselves, that we are better than we are, we are free to receive his forgiveness and forgive ourselves. We can put down the masks we wear and know that we are accepted as we are. Hebrews 4:13 states that "Nothing in all creation is hidden from God's sight."

Question 13. Some principles are: confession to God; don't hide from God or allow despair to overwhelm you; remember God knows all there is to know about you; humble yourself before God and before your friends; confess to a friend; receive God's forgiveness in full — go through the whole situation with him and ask for forgiveness; consciously forgive yourself also.

Now or later. As you finish the booklet, you might want to plan an extra session for people to share what spoke to them most deeply and have time to pray for one another. Keep the cross of Christ central during this time. You might like to sing or read out some verses to highlight all that Jesus has done for us.

Christine Platt became a Christian while training to be a nurse in London. This led her to Africa, to work with the Navigators as a missionary on the Cote d'Ivoire. She has studied French and creative writing, and has written articles for a number of Christian journals, including the Baptist Times *and* Woman Alive. LifeBuilder Forgiveness *is her first book. Christine lives in Cardiff, Wales.*

What Should We Study Next?

A good place to start your study of Scripture would be with a book study. Many groups begin with a Gospel such as *Mark* (20 studies by Jim Hoover) or *John* (26 studies by Douglas Connelly). These guides are divided into two parts so that if twenty or twenty-six weeks seems like too much to do at once, the group can feel free to do half and take a break with another topic. Later you might want to come back to it. You might prefer to try a shorter letter. *Philippians* (9 studies by Donald Baker), *Ephesians* (13 studies by Andrew T. and Phyllis J. Le Peau) and *1 & 2 Timothy and Titus* (12 studies by Peter Sommer) are good options. If you want to vary your reading with an Old Testament book, consider *Ecclesiastes* (12 studies by Bill and Teresa Syrios) for a challenging and exciting study.

There are a number of interesting topical LifeBuilder studies as well. Here are some options for filling three or four quarters of a year:

Basic Discipleship
Christian Beliefs, 12 studies by Stephen D. Eyre
Christian Character, 12 studies by Andrea Sterk & Peter Scazzero
Christian Disciplines, 12 studies by Andrea Sterk & Peter Scazzero
Evangelism, 12 studies by Rebecca Pippert & Ruth Siemens

Building Community
Christian Community, 12 studies by Rob Suggs
Fruit of the Spirit, 9 studies by Hazel Offner
Spiritual Gifts, 12 studies by Charles & Anne Hummel

Character Studies
New Testament Characters, 12 studies by Carolyn Nystrom
Old Testament Characters, 12 studies by Peter Scazzero
Old Testament Kings, 12 studies by Carolyn Nystrom
Women of the Old Testament, 12 studies by Gladys Hunt

The Trinity
Meeting God, 12 studies by J. I. Packer
Meeting Jesus, 13 studies by Leighton Ford
Meeting the Spirit, 12 studies by Douglas Connelly